THE
BABIES

D1439449

First published in 1989 by
Cornerhouse Publications,
70, Oxford Street,
Manchester M1 5NH
061 228 7621

ISBN 0 948797 60 6

DESIGN
Christopher Halls

PRINTED BY
Jackson Wilson

THE
BABIES

photographs by

SUE PACKER

Text by Martin Caiger-Smith and Bill Jay

CORNERHOUSE
PUBLICATIONS

MANCHESTER

for

DAVID HURN AND SARAH RICKETTS

A child, barely a year of age (at a guess) stares fixedly out at us from the small frame. She (or he?) wears an intricate dress of lace, details faded in the pale sepia of the hundred year-old print. Straight-backed, she perches on the corner of the photographer's outsize armchair, in the gloomy surround of some Victorian studio. A slight blur marks the shift of her hand during the long exposure.

Those who first admired this portrait would have been family and friends, to whom the child had a name, a voice. The portrait would have been commissioned by her proud family out of desire, still almost universal to this day, to record for posterity the features of their child at this early stage of its life. They may have judged this a good likeness, displayed it with pride or labelled it with others in the family album.

Now, a century later, this image, like thousands of others found in junkshops, old albums and photographic collections, appears in a different light. The young sitter is unknown to us, anonymous and long dead. We can establish no personal relationship with them, as we can with most portraits, of family, friends or well-known personalities. Despite, or perhaps because of this, these portraits can hold for us a particular and intense fascination, a poignant otherworldliness which grips our attention. Part of this is the dignity conferred by time, and part their enigmatic quality - they have the sense of an obscure historical document, their details pointing to clues in a mystery that can never be solved. We find ourselves trying to build a picture of an unknown life, but they remain at a distance, aloof, posing more questions than they give answers.

Sue Packer has a large and growing collection of these Victorian portraits, swelled continually by interested friends all over the world. Her fascination for them gave her the inspiration for this work.

Switch to one of Sue Packer's photographs. In dead centre is a child dressed in flowing christening gown propped carefully on a floral patterned sofa amid a heap of plush cushions. Behind her, an elaborately framed photograph, a pair of china dogs, a leaded window pane and the trees beyond suggest a rural or suburban home and a middle-class background, but nothing more is stated. The child, still and alone with the photographer, positioned carefully within the intricately composed frame, fixes her gaze on the camera.

Sue Packer does not identify her subjects or locations; nor does she work to commission. These are not 'portraits' - her choices are her own, her interests less in pleasing parents than in creating strong images with formal power which convey the compelling sense of strangeness that she herself found in looking at these relics from a different age.

She restricts herself to the passive subject. All are between three months and one year of age - old enough for their eyes to focus, still too young to walk unaided away from the camera. At the outset, Packer realised that she was entering difficult territory. Though one of the most widespread of photographic subjects, child portraiture has seldom been given serious attention. It is burdened by a weight of tradition and overwhelming sameness, trapped between the poles of the amateur snapshot and the mawkish sentimental code of the high street studio portrait. She is virtually alone in her attempt to adopt and adapt the genre for her own ends, to remove it from the domain of the family to a more public sphere.

As in her other series, *Tintern Portraits* and *Cheltenham Ladies' College*, Packer's working method is painstaking, based on detailed research and orchestration of setting, and on a strong collaboration between herself and her subject, which allows for improvisation but leaves her in strict control of the final image. This discipline and sense of formality is just as crucial in this new series. The line between success and failure - between ordinariness and the special quality she is searching for - is thin, and the distinction all too easy for her to recognise. For however different her intent, she is still working within a recognised genre, perilously close to the many traps which can lead to a mediocre image, to the sentimental, the banal and the clichéd. Many attempts fail, many images she rejects. Those which satisfy her, those which work, have an undeniable force.

Each session can be long and arduous, each encounter is a new and different challenge. Packer substitutes the baby's home environment for the props of the Victorian studio, picking up on telling detail which enlivens the image, and maybe drops a clue or two about the infant's family, life - even its destiny? Any object or location maybe pressed into service. An idea often springs from the parents' views of their own children - or she may turn for inspiration to the family album, creating a doubling of imagery which casts a characteristic pose in a new, sharper light. The final result is always tightly constructed, often with a calculated symmetry, at times echoing the formal pose of a particular Victorian portrait image, and often drawing on a vast range of sources in the broader tradition of portraiture, from painting as much as photography. The child, in bonnet and lace dress which is splayed across the picture so she appears almost to float, conjures images of a handmaiden in an Elizabethan or a Spanish court painting...

In another image a child, cross-legged and perfectly poised beside a vase of roses, sports plastic specs and a moustache. Another wilts beneath the weight of her mother's wig. Packer's subjects are dressed up, trussed up by adults, lodged and wedged and suspended. In the final hard-won image, however, all effort is concealed, the scene appears remarkably unforced. The babies are (for that split second) immobile, very few smile or register emotion. They may be surrounded by the playthings of childhood, but they are not playing. That Victorian maxim comes to mind that every child is a little adult. All confront the camera directly, and many manage to convey a strangely adult composure. These children, unknown to us, as yet unmarked by the experiences of life and too young, surely, to project a conscious image of themselves, still reveal a strong individuality and a personal presence. For they are more than mere objects before the camera; they are self-possessed, displaying a degree of awareness and a strange complicity in the whole procedure which must be as much apparent as real.

They appear to enter into the role-playing, even to throw in a few surprises of their own. Packer's distinctive vision forces us to look at them in a new and different way. Her pictures are dispassionate, and difficult to characterise - at times both solemn and humorous, comforting and yet 'strange' - their strength lies in this tension which prompts in us an equivocal reaction. We are torn between the formal elegance, the public presence of the photograph and our recollections of 'similar' images from our own past. They provide an echo, these babies in adult guise, of our own childhood, largely remembered through images, only incompletely, and with an adult perception - for though we can all recall something of our early years, we have long forgotten what it *feels* like to be a child.

Packer succeeds in pulling this familiar subject matter into fresh and unfamiliar territory, linking it with a broader tradition of photography. She brings a sense of Diane Arbus's fierce fascinated gaze into the child's bedroom; an infant slumped in his nursery chair recalls the comfortable satisfaction of one of August Sander's bankers. But such links, though they give her work an edge, should not be stretched too far. Sue Packer works within a strictly domestic sphere. Hers is no conscious project of social documentation. Her focus is narrow and personal, the visual evidence she scatters around is too enigmatic and fragmentary to suggest any idea of a new social survey. The variety of her images reflects instead her relentless search for new visual possibilities, new situations to resolve. Sue Packer's original fascination has deepened as the series developed. You can almost see her finishing a session with two twins in their fifties-style living room, and hearing with enthusiasm the news of a woman in the next village who has just given birth to triplets...

Martin Caiger-Smith

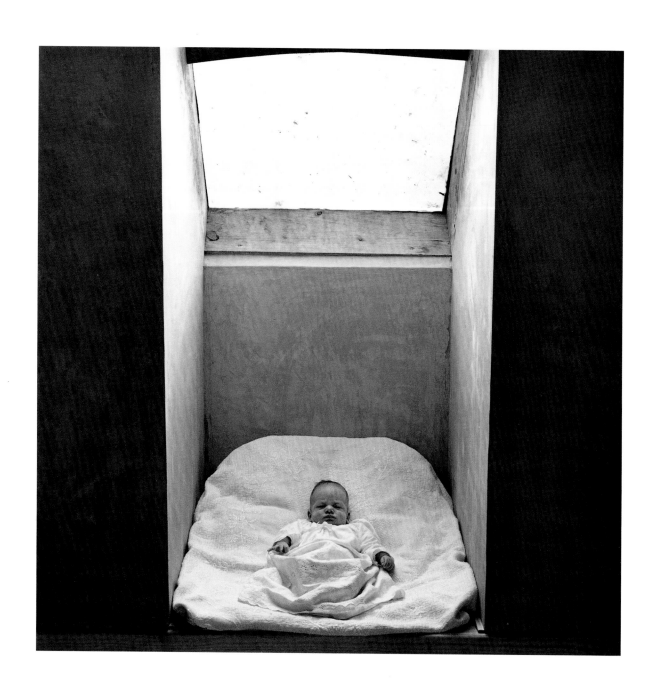

INFANTRY TACTICS

At the peak of the Victorian Age when well-bred young ladies were encouraged to cultivate the arts of "Refinement" (which meant any activity which was singularly useless), women were never the less encouraged to enter the ranks of professional photography. The photographic press often carried articles by (male) writers urging women to open their own studios and one of them did even assert that "the ladies now at the head of photographic establishments, and doing the operating themselves, give evidence of an ability quite equal to, if not surpassing, that of the best of masculine competitors". Another (male) writer attested that the profession of photography "is one in which there is no sexual hostility to their employment". "There is no adequate reason," he stated in 1873, "why the number should not be largely increased."

There was a good reason why women were valued as photographers: by far the most frequent visitors to portraiture studios were ladies and babies. With both types of clients, the female photographer excelled. She was deemed better able to provide ladies with advice on hair and dress styles and she would be encouraged to physically arrange the pose, adjust drapery and finishing touches to the ladies' coiffure - all of which would have

①

"Yes he was a precious angel! - He sall have his picture - picture taken."

②

The field of action.

③

"You must expect the first three or four pictures to be failures. We will first quiet him down!"

④

"If his attention can be arrested."

been considered impertinent if attempted by a man.

Baby photographs demanded an extraordinary amount of understanding, skill, tact and patience on behalf of the operator in a 19th century studio. At no stage of the process was patience more demanded than during the efforts required to keep the baby still during the tediously long exposure.

This was particularly true in the early years of the medium when the daguerreotype predominated and exposure times were often measured in minutes rather than fractions of a second. Adult sitters suffered the seemingly interminable exposures with their heads rigidly clamped in order to prevent movement. Babies could not be brutalised in the same way, and sharp daguerreotypes of infants are relatively rare. It is often asserted, with some justification, that a sharp image of a baby in a daguerreotype means the infant was dead. Such post-mortem baby daguerreotypes were common, especially in America, when infant mortality rates were so high. Photographers prided themselves on posing the baby, often on the mother's lap, so that the infant looked asleep or even alive (by pinning open the lids and injecting the eyes with drops of glycerine.

From the early 1850s, the daguerreotype was giving way to the collodion or wet-plate process. Although that reduced exposure times, they were still agonisingly drawn out - up to thirty seconds. Head clamps were still required for adults, and still impractical for infants.

So how did the photographer obtain a sharp image of a restless, squirming baby during the exposure?

One photographic magazine suggested giving the sitter a good dose of laudanum, a tincture of opium (the Victorian's aspirin). The writer remarked that the opium "will effectually prevent the sitters from being conscious of themselves, or of the camera, or of anything else". "They become, " he congratulated himself, "most delightfully tractable."

Punch magazine (1864) also contributed its own ideas on "The Best Mode of Keeping Babies Still for the Photographic Sitting". It suggested chloroform, which had recently become popular as an anesthetic.

The same writer concluded that "if the mothers would only stay away, there would be no difficulty, as all babies were exactly alike, and a single type could be reproduced from an old picture." Like much facetious writing, there was a strong element of truth in this remark. In an age when clients were a lot less sophisticated about photography, cheap-jack photographers did substitute a "stock" picture of a baby of approximately the right age if the actual one was a technical failure.

A few years later a photographer from Danbury took the idea to its logical conclusion. He reasoned that his clients could not fidget during the exposure if they were insensible, and he promised to revolutionise the business of portraiture by the introduction of a gas which rendered the sitter unconscious during the taking of the picture. He issued cards announcing: "Photographs in all styles without pain." In an age when a visit to a photographer's studio was no more appreciated than a visit to a dentist, these solutions of

"Rest after the 13th failure.
Interval for refreshment."

"Perhaps his nurse may
be able to controll him"

The 17th failure brings with
it a feeling of despair.

Possibly he will sit still, if alone.

The result not satisfactory.

gassing and drugging seemed eminently reasonable.

Most portraitists, however, did not resort to such extremes. they relied on patience and efforts to distract the attentions of the baby. There are many suggestions in the 19th century photographic press on methods offered by individual operators for the distraction of infants. Some seemed more time-consuming and impractical than the effort warranted, others were brutal, many were ingenious. A particularly clever idea was to dip the baby's hands in treacle and the plunge one of them into a bag of feathers. In theory, the child's attention was riveted on the act of picking feathers from one sticky hand to the other, "giving you ample opportunity to make an artistic exposure".

More practical was to amuse the child with a real, or mechanical animal. One American portraitist trained a monkey to actually make the exposure: the *New York Sun* stated that this is "the first time that an ape has been responsibly engaged in the service of art". A photographer called Davis trained a canary - not to make the exposure but to sing on command. When about to remove the lens cap from the camera, the bird "at once bursts forth in sweet song" and "the sitter forgets all about the headrest, the trying light, the wearisomeness of keeping a fixed position, etc . . ." For those photographers with less aptitude for animal training, photographic dealers could supply mechanical birds which opened their beaks and warbled when a pneumatic bulb was squeezed. These gadgets were very popular and no doubt led to the photographic cliché "watch the birdie.

Even less demanding of the photographer's attention were the camera stands used, and distributed, by a Mr Spicer of Birmingham. He was an expert in stuffing kittens and constructed stands and even picture frames featuring his art, for which the demand was "practically unlimited". No doubt the RSPCA would object to a revival of such photographic props although they still seem more tasteful than the attention-seeking technique of one photographer in the American West, who would remove a huge quid of tobacco from his mouth and hurl it against the wall, higher than his head, and take the exposure while the fascinated child watched masticated tobacco dribble down the wall.

The difficulties, and frustrations, of attempting to photograph babies in a Victorian studio were legendary. Scores of tales were told with which all photographers, every-where, could empathise. A typical anecdote concerned a photographer who had been trying for two hours to take a satisfactory picture, without success, and in his frustration hurled a lens at the infant. As soon as the magistrate heard the circumstances, he interrupted: "You are discharged. I used to be a photographer myself".

Throughout the 19th century, as these anecdotes will indicate, babies were considered the supreme test of a photographer's mettle, skill and patience. It is significant that when George G. Rockwood of New York issued a booklet in 1874-5 (as something to read while the sitter waited for his/her turn in front of the lens) *all* the illustrations concern the frustration of photographing babies, culminating in the photographer stamping in anger on the final ruined plate. In the light of these illustrations, and suggested by the booklets' title, *Rockwood's Photographic Art-illery Manual and Infantry Tactics*, it would be reasonable to assume that the text dealt at length with the portraiture of babies.

Ha[ppy] thought! Try brute force.

2d Happy thought! Rewards.

Last experiment – Punishment.

Defeat.

Retreat.

Unfortunately, it contains only one short paragraph on the subject:

Children should always be dressed in light colours or white, and should never be taken to the gallery after two P.M. Never attempt to coerce a child to sit for its picture. If it won't sit willingly, it should be brought again at some other time. Never coax a child with sweetmeats or give it anything to play with during the sitting. With your child bring plenty of patience, *and we will endeavour to exercise a becoming degree of that grace.*

This would be reasonable advice even today, more than 100 years later.

Babies still comprise one of the most difficult subjects for photographers, in spite of the enormous increases in the speed and sophistication of our films and cameras, because the time-honoured attributes of skill, tact and patience are still essential prerequisites for success.

Sue Packer must have these characteristics to an extraordinary degree, in order to produce such a remarkable set of photographs. She is the descendant of a long line of committed, and often unappreciated, female photographers. They - and George Rockwood - would have been proud of her.

Bill Jay

Illustrations from Rockwood's Photographic Art-illery Manual, 1874 - 5 by George G. Rockwood.

Daguerrotype of a young girl, c. 1850, from The Art of the Daguerrotype by Stephen Richter, published by Viking.

Martin Caiger-Smith is currently Exhibitions Organiser at
the Photographers' Gallery, London.

Bill Jay is Professor of Art History at Arizona State University
where he initiated the History of Photography programme.
He is a world renowned photo historian and writer.

SUE PACKER

1974 - 77 BA (Honours) in Fine Art, Newport College of Art and Design, South Wales

1977 - 79 MA in Photography, Royal College of Art, London

1981 - 86 Freelance portrait photographer; work for *The Times, Observer, Daily Telegraph, Good Housekeeping, Over 21, Time Out*

1984 -   Part time lecturer, Documentary course, Newport College of Art and Design

SELECTED EXHIBITIONS

1983 *Contemporary European Portraiture*, Northlight Gallery, Arizona, USA

1985 *Sue Packer: Tintern Portraits*, Ffotogallery Cardiff and tour

European Woman Photographers Today, Torino Fotografia, Italy

Portrait Photography by British Photographers 1935 - 1985, Impressions Gallery, York

Image and Exploration, Photographers' Gallery, London

1987 *Realities Revisited: 15 British Photographers*, Centre Saidye Bronfman, Montreal, Canada

1988 *The Wheel of Life. Photographs by Anne Noggle and Sue Packer*, Photographers' Gallery, London

1989 *Sue Packer: A Portrait of Cheltenham Ladies' College*, touring show

1989 *Sue Packer: Baby Sittings*, touring show

WORK PUBLISHED IN

A Day in the Life of London, 1984

A Week in the Life of Ireland, 1986

Photographers' Encyclopaedia International, 1839 - present

Val Williams, Woman Photographers: The Other Observers, 1900 to the Present

Acknowledgements

Martin Caiger-Smith
Bill Jay
Colin Jacobson
Georgie Meadows
Debbie Howells
Nina Phelps
Margaret Jones

Sue Packer's <u>Babies</u> portrait series
was undertaken with the support of a
commission from the Photographer's
Gallery London. An Exhibition of the
work entitled "Sue Packer: Baby Sittings' is
currently being toured nationally by the gallery.

*Original prints from this book
can be purchased from:*

DIRK SWERINGEN
28 KINGSHOLM ROAD
GLOUCESTER
GL1 3AU
ENGLAND